18

Preparing our younger selves for an unpredictable future

By Toby LaVigne

In Memory of my Mom, our first and most important teacher, who taught us;

That anything worth doing is worth doing well
Don't take yourself too seriously
Be Brave
and
Remember that sometimes the greatest gift is to give others a chance to give

Preface

In the early 1900's an innovation came to the fore that would end up transforming the world in unimaginable ways. It was the internal combustion engine. This innovation was the beginning of a natural and predictable cycle that has occurred for all of man's time here on earth and for billions and billions of years before us.

The cycle that you can see in the illustration below goes in a clockwise direction; first, there is a break through technological innovation, which transforms social relationships and business structures and finally leads to new political configurations.

21st CENTURY BREAKDOWN

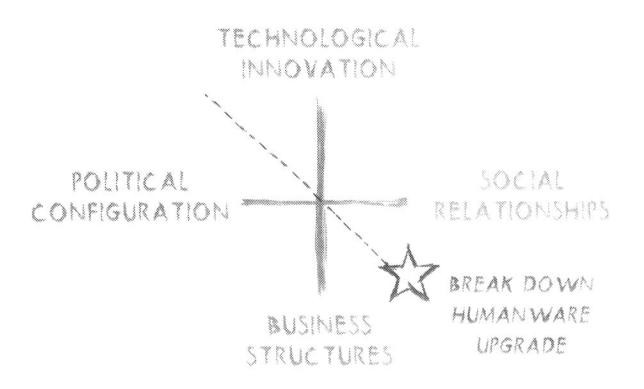

TECHNOLOGICAL INNOVATION

POLITICAL CONFIGURATION

SOCIAL RELATIONSHIPS

BUSINESS STRUCTURES

BREAK DOWN
HUMANWARE
UPGRADE

One of the earliest and certainly one of the most impactful applications of the engine was in farming. Farming at the time was an enormously labor intensive activity. So much so that large landowners sublet parcels to families who in turn earned a living on the farm.

The tractor eliminated the need for large numbers of farm hands and before long, the landowners stopped subletting their land to individual families, and an enormous number of farming families were 'tractored' off the fields and into the cities.

This deeply affected social relationships. Thriving farm towns withered and America moved off of the front porch and into city life. No longer needing large numbers of children to work the farm, family size quickly began to shrink.

The engine further impacted business structures. It enabled Henry Ford to build the Tin Lizzie and along with other manufacturers, employed displaced farmers by the thousands. With so many emerging consumers, the general store transformed from an order counter at the back of the store to a cash register at the front of what became the grocery store. The internal combustion engine literally gave birth to mass consumerism.

Finally, all of this change necessitated political adjustments. The loss of the small town that 'took care of its own' created challenges that needed to be addressed by the city. And as women got out of the isolation of the farm, their interest in politics grew, and soon we amended our constitution to allow women to vote.

What we can see from this cycle is that although the transitions weren't always seamless, society did move forward in a clockwise direction, and an unprecedented increase in the quality of life ensued.

Today we can see that we have another major break through innovation; the Internet. And it too is transforming social relationships in profound ways. Social media is enabling people to interact across the globe in real time. The Internet has the potential to transform how we do everything.

But there is one very big problem. In the last cycle, when workers got 'tractored' off the farm, there were factory jobs that any able-bodied man or women could perform with a minimum of on the job training. Not this time.

This time people are getting 'Interneted' out of their jobs and there aren't any 'off the shelf' replacements waiting for them AND they don't have the capability to create their own.

In the last economic cycle others externally imposed our professional identities upon us, but in this cycle our professional identities must be *internally exposed* by us.

This time, workers, especially the next generation are expected to jump from dependent employees to interdependent contractors using the education designed for the last cycle.

21st CENTURY BREAKDOWN

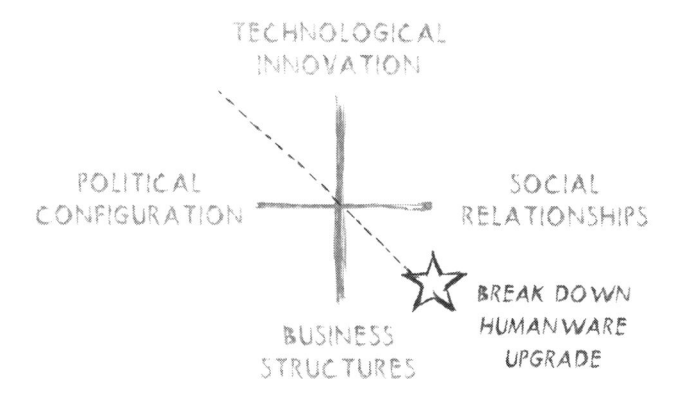

```
              TECHNOLOGICAL
               INNOVATION
                   |
        \          |
         \         |
  POLITICAL  \     |         SOCIAL
CONFIGURATION ─────┼─────  RELATIONSHIPS
                   |  \
                   |   ☆  BREAK DOWN
                   |       HUMANWARE
               BUSINESS     UPGRADE
              STRUCTURES
```

This new requirement to participate in the economy and to prosper is not just a problem for the next generation, it's a problem for businesses who also have to adapt, it's a problem for a government that is being blamed for the breakdown, and it's a problem for parents, grandparents and tax payers who must suffer the consequences.

The gap between what the new economy requires of it's participants and the business status quo is stalling economies and causing increasing unrest; the Arab Spring, protests in Turkey and Brazil, as well as our own 99% demonstrations are all symptoms of the same problem.

Unfortunately, we are not moving forward, we're going backwards. Our greatest institutions; our government, banks, academia, medicine, large corporations and media alike are all moving counter-clockwise to Political Configuration. As a society we are trying to rejigger the system hoping that somehow more prosperity will result.

It's like being at the end of a tube of toothpaste, without realizing it. Our previous successes at squeezing have deluded us into thinking that if we just keep coming up with new ways to squeeze, then prosperity will be restored. Unfortunately the less that comes out, the more anxious we get, and the more anxious we get, the harder we squeeze.

This is a negative feedback loop that WILL NOT CREATE PROSPERITY for our children or for our society. The key to stopping this feedback loop lies in the preparation of our next generation.

Table of Contents

Introduction 1
Antifragility 4
Assume that College isn't an option 6
13 7
Self-Awareness 8
No Tests 9
Peer Reputation 10
Portfolios 11
Journal 12
Four types of learning 13
Don't know nothing bout history 16
STEM 17
Big picture 18
Under schedule 19
No homework 20
Ethic of Excellence 21
Be an adaptable learning organization 23
The 3 R's 24
Learning happens to us when we're doing
    something else 25
Understand vs know 27
10,000 hours 28
Talent 30
We can't do anything we set our minds to 31

Ideas worth spreading	32
Cloud	34
Kill your Television	35
We've become too PC (politically correct)	36
Be in touch with nature often	37
Meditation	39
Power Nap	40
Nutrition	41
Fitness	43
Sports	44
Learning Evolution	45
No more teachers	46
Learning leadership	48
You get 10 minutes	51
Group accomplishment	52
Collaboration is not cheating	54
Ethics	55
Integrity	56
Project group learning mentors	57
Class size	58
Engage the village	59
Parents must walk the talk	60
How long should a school day be?	61
Scheduling and breaks	62
Learning and humiliation are the same	63
Tough Love and hard things	64
Turn off the lights	66

Everyone stands watch 67
Manners 68
Resolving conflict.. 69
18 70
Education never ends.. 71
College, one more time for good measure 72
The Vision 75
Toby LaVigne – Jupiter, FL 76
Resources 78

Introduction

The purpose of this book is to create a context for designing a completely new approach to preparation for adulthood. My intention is to question educational authority and spark an educational design discussion and a movement to prepare our next generation with the tools to thrive in an unknowable future.

This book is broken up into a number of 'posts' designed to focus our attention on various aspects of education. The posts are by no means an exhaustive list of relevant topics, but they provide the basis of our education philosophy.

When it comes to education we all want what is best for our children. But what is best? We know what it *has been.* The 'common sense' path to 'the best' education *has been* to get good grades and test scores so that you can get into the 'best' college or university, so that you will get the best jobs, earn the most money and live the best life.

There is a saying, "The map is not the territory". Which simply means that sometimes looking at a map of what we *think* is the territory prevents us from seeing possibilities that are not on the map.

The traditional map that describes what education should accomplish, where it should go, and how to get there, prevent us from seeing vast amounts of rich territory that hold greater opportunities for our children's development, and in turn our societies evolution.

I do not claim to have the ability to map the future of education. I DO claim to have an intense commitment to our children's future and in turn our society. To this end, allow me to suggest some 'ground rules' for this discussion;

- Small changes generally don't scare us. If education needed small changes, you wouldn't be reading this book. **Remind yourself and others that the 'right' solutions can not be known in advance**, we must simply commit to moving forward, together, with a powerful curiosity to find vastly better means of learning and vastly better means of measuring our results.

- Children who participate in a school that is itself a learning organism, will develop a profound ability to deal with change, cooperation, and conflict resolution. **Consider whether you are willing to be the change that you want to see.**

- Read this book, not as a critic or with an intent to defend your path, but out of a commitment to the generations behind you that are entering a entirely new world economy than you did.

- Ask yourself, "Given the new realities of technology, how can we create the most powerful learning experience for our children?"
- And look for the connection between the problems faced in our education system and the problems faced by families, businesses and government as they are all connected.

I hope this book enables you to see the issues facing us today in a new light and that it inspires you to support new solutions.

Antifragility

Antifragility is a term that is being introduced and made popular by best selling author Nassim Nicholas Taleb, author of Fooled by Randomness, Black Swan, and now Antifragility.

Antifragility is a word that is long overdue in our vocabulary. When we think of the opposite of fragile, words like robust or resilient or unbreakable probably come to mind. But there is no such thing as 'unbreakable' and our belief in the myth of indestructibility and total security is paradoxically making us *more* vulnerable and *more* fragile.

We can't predict or securitize the future.

Antifragility on the other hand is a natural system that we can leverage to increase our ability to withstand whatever the future brings us. Antifragile systems and people actually become stronger as a result of challenge.

Antifragility is the phenomenon that got us humans where we are today. It is both unnatural and unsafe to abandon the system that has ensured our survival for thousands of years.

As Nassim says in Antifragility, "We didn't get where we are thanks to the silly notion of resilience.

And, what's worse, we didn't get where we are today thanks to policy makers—but thanks to the appetite for risks and errors of a certain class of people we need to encourage, protect, and respect."

In this book I will argue that we need to raise and educate our children to be 'antifragile'; to teach them to embrace, encourage, and respect the process of learning by making numerous mistakes that have small harm, so that they and our society can withstand the unpredictable events that will inevitably bring great harm.

The pace of change is accelerating, complexity is accelerating, and even the acceleration of both is accelerating. The solution to a rapidly changing and increasingly complex world is NOT more complex systems. These attempts at reducing risk actually INCREASE our vulnerability not DECREASE it.

I argue that our education system is making our children and has made our society more and more fragile in part because it rewards knowing the 'known' and punishes failures.

I argue that our educational system has deluded us into believing that risk can be managed and that the path to a successful future can be taught and tested.

This is rubbish.

Assume that College isn't an option

First of all, if the college diploma were a stock, fewer investors would be buying it. With the exception of pursuing some specific fields of study, college is a dubious investment, and even *then* the economics are dicey.

Some say that college is an important growing up experience. I say that anyone who engages in real life pursuits from the age of 18 to 22 is going to 'grow up'. Colleges have become Peter Pan Never Never Lands competing to outdo each other with better food, dorms and buildings.

Investing 4 years of your life and getting into enough debt to buy a house is a heavy price to pay.

We would approach education from 13-18 much more differently if there weren't a make believe backstop called college.

Which leads us to…

13

When George Washington was 14 he surveyed the state of Virginia. Cultures that believe that 13 is the beginning of adulthood have it right. We owe it to our kids to give them greater challenges, to give them the opportunity to build confidence and self-esteem to face the real world.

And we owe it to our children to give them a powerful rite of passage between childhood and adulthood. Our current approach creates an expectation that students have until as late as 29 or even later to 'get serious'.

What if the goal was to produce an 18 year old that was fully capable of landing on their feet and prospering?

Self-Awareness

When a teenager is asked what they want to contribute in life, the response shouldn't be staring at their shoes. There is no better time than school to discover who you are and what you can contribute.

The student doesn't have to know exactly how they are going to manifest it, but we owe it to our students to not send them into adulthood without a clue.

Just because most adults are unconscious, doesn't mean that it's ok. Schools that graduate students that don't have a very firm grasp on who they are and what they stand for have failed.

I give them an F.

No Tests

As an employer, I don't care what a candidate memorized (and quickly forgot) 10 years ago or even 1 year ago. Teaching to tests is lazy, ineffective, and too frequently irrelevant.

What is far more powerful and relevant is to practice debriefing with peer feedback. The practice of giving and receiving feedback causes more upsets in and out of the workplace than we can possibly count, but it is also THE most powerful source of true learning.

Giving and receiving feedback is a skill that takes practice. The ability to hear it and learn from it is a muscle that requires development. The greatest breakdown we face as a society right now is our inability to adapt to the pace of change.

Filling in circles with a No. 2 pencil can never replace the ability to face and learn from breakdowns.

Learning to learn is the goal, not memorization.

If we don't have tests in the traditional form, how will the market know if your child is a truly curious, ambitious, continuous learner?…

Peer Reputation

What we all want to know when we first meet someone is this; Will this person do what they say they will do?

The market reputation of highly educated and licensed professionals is not very good. If you don't believe me, ask some friends to assess some recent transactions with a; doctor, lawyer, contractor, real estate broker, investment professional, banker. Etc.

There are two ways to answer the question of whether someone will do what they say they will;

1. Look at their track record
2. Try a project with them and find out

What students need are;

- Increasingly challenging situations to forge their capacity to accomplish
- A mechanism to communicate accomplishments and capabilities
- The ability to present themselves and negotiate for their value

Which leads me to…

Portfolios

Students need to accomplish real world tasks and collect demonstrations of their best work over time as a means of showing what they are capable of when they face the market.

Tests and test papers tell me the candidate was good at taking tests, but they don't show me what they are capable of in terms of real life work.

By the time a student is 18 years old, they should have accumulated a portfolio demonstration of their capability, which will already represent their 'core offer' to the market.

There is no reason why an 18 year old should need 5 more years 'experience' before they can become a powerful contributor to an organization. They should be ready to contribute right out of the box

Journal

One of the most powerful means of self-reflection and growth is to journal. I don't go anywhere without my journal. It is by my side at my desk, and it accompanies me everywhere I go.

It is my 'white board' for illustrating ideas. It is where I record new ideas, commitments, and observations. It is an essential tool in my ongoing discovery process.

I wish that I had developed the journaling habit in the 1st grade. Instead of staring out the window I could have been drafting my masterpiece. Help students develop the journaling habit, and create time for them to review it so that they can develop a strong sense of how they learn and who they are.

Life without a journal is like diving to the bottom of the ocean without a camera.

Four types of learning

Learning to BE, learning to DO, learning to KNOW, and learning to TRANSACT.

Learning to **BE** is essential. Knowing who you are, where you are coming from and the dent you intend to make in your universe are incredibly powerful assets. It's humbling how many adults do not know who they are. Not knowing who we are and what our powerful contribution is leaves us adrift and anxious – a condition that makes us vulnerable to a wide variety of distractions.

We can do better for our children.

Learning to **DO** has to do with developing skills. (see 10,000 hours) This involves time and practice. There are a number of skills mentioned in this book that students traditionally get very little practice at and it shows up big time in adulthood.

Perhaps the biggest downfall of this is that we are producing adults who don't think these skills are that important or 'learnable', so they don't work on them and a lot of suffering ensues.

Learning to **KNOW** is about facts; quick, what is the square root of 625?

Two things on 'knowing';

First, the half-life of memorized facts is about only a day or two. We all know this yet we insist on marching kids through texts books and giving quizzes and tests to evaluate their ability to memorize facts that will be forgotten in an extremely short period of time unless they become embedded through necessity and interest.

Second, we should be aiming for more understanding and a bit less knowing. My dedication to learning has enabled me to *understand* how a lot of things work (conceptually), but I don't *know* how to *do* them all, and that's as it should be. My understanding of a wide range of subjects greatly supports my ability to understand new things and to empathize with others.

Learning to TRANSACT. This is the biggest miss of the four. The number one thing that every human must do from birth to death is transact. Imagine if some alien observers came down here to earth to grab some lunch. And while lunching, they observed our parenting, marriages, work interactions, and our government. Now imagine they get their check and one of those comment cards. What would they write?

Humans seem to be constantly jockeying for position at each other's expense. They are clever and all seem to have significant contributions to make, but don't seem to have a clue what their contribution is, when to provide it or how to negotiate a reciprocal exchange for it.

And the oddest part of it all is that they keep doing the same thing expecting a different result. Why are they so surprised when they don't get the life they intended?! Half of the population gets cancer and heart disease, the environment is a mess, the political process is embarrassing; there are lawyers and disagreements everywhere. These creatures are insane.

Our inability to give and receive feedback, to ask for what we truly want, to establish and defend our own standards, and to negotiate for our value is a crime that starts in the 1st grade. We can't afford to squander the most impressionable time in our children's development to establish the ability to transact.

Don't know nothing bout history

Some people lament that, "kids today don't know their history". The *history*, these people are often referring to is primarily composed of the events that *they lived* through. Kids today won't have any problem *knowing* about 911, the housing collapse, or the early days of the ipad.

Beyond relatively recent history, most people (of all ages) don't *know* their history. To be fair, there is A LOT to know and it grows every year. I remember taking history class where we read a chapter, had a quiz, read a few more chapters then had a test.

The emphasis was on memorizing facts I completely missed the opportunity to *understand* the big picture – a gap that I have worked hard to fill as an adult.

We can make history fun and relevant by understanding the macro phases of human existence. Where was the power? Where was the innovation? How was it applied? Misapplied? Why? Where was the suffering? What can we learn?

STEM

Science, Technology, and Math are a hot subject these days. I keep hearing that the US lags the rest of the world in these areas. I don't doubt that we do, but I'm concerned about how we are interpreting our test score results and what's most important. Here are a few of my observations as a technologist who has spent a fair amount of time in the commercial world of finance (math), biotech (science), and software (technology).

I want our children to develop a broad and working understanding of technologies, their applications, and next areas for exploration. I want them to experience it hands on with real life projects.

We should be more concerned about STEM *ignorance*. Adults who lack STEM competence are often missing the ability to ask questions and to understand how to make important decisions about their medical care, their nutrition, or the environmental consequences of their consumption. Are tests measuring this?

STEM ignorance threatens democracy. The decisions that we must make as voters are getting more and more complex, and STEM ignorance plays a large role in voter apathy. When only a small percentage of a society truly understands what is going on, then it ceases to be a democracy. Again, the issue of *knowing vs understanding*.

Big picture

When we observe people debating issues and making decisions we can see that we default to the short-term and to self-interest. There are a lot of reasons for this, but one important antidote is the ability to SEE the bigger picture. Today's sound bite, video bite, black and white media approach persists because we let it.

People that can look at and see the bigger picture intentionally make different media choices so that they CAN see the bigger picture. This too is a skill and a habit, which our education system does not develop in students. Heads down in a textbook stressed about tonight's homework and Friday's test obscures the big picture and you can watch the adult consequences on tonight's news.

Under schedule

Measuring student and educational success by how much content we can stuff in our kid's heads and testing to it creates a time urgency that requires a dense schedule. "We don't have enough time! Hurry up….hurry here….then hurry over there…oh God we're falling behind…more homework, more lectures, more tests!"

This is a lesson in scarcity that breeds a society that is anxious, selfish, greedy, exhausted, confused and unhappy.

Learning and development have nothing to do with *quantity* of time and everything to do with *quality* of time. Focus on creating a learning experience that is based upon economy -doing more with less- instead of efficiency. The market doesn't care how many meetings, emails and tasks the adult can accomplish, it only cares about results.

No homework

Going home at night to stare at text books for 2 to 4 hours…really!? What on earth does this accomplish? If students need 1 to 2 hours per subject per day in addition to the 1 hour of class time, what the heck is happening in class?

There are times when we need to put in some extra time after regular school and work hours, but they must by definition be the exception not the norm or we're missing the point of life. Homework is delegating the schools job and it interrupts family time, time to master something, and time to explore without any boundaries.

'Homework' time needs to be reallocated not to leisure time, but to 'other exploration'.

Ethic of Excellence

Under scheduling does not mean *easy*. Quite the opposite. Students need to be challenged and they need to hold themselves and their teammates to higher standards. But when time is crunched standards are always the first thing to go. If we want students to truly achieve great things, we can't wait until after college to raise their standards. They must *live* in a climate that has an ethic of excellence about it from day one.

This isn't just about student expectations; this must begin with the learning leaders and parents. This won't make me popular, but my observation is that too many 'teachers' and parents don't hold themselves to a high enough standard. And anyone who has studied organizations and teams knows that leaders always set the high water mark.

The biggest failing of our education system is the low standards set by the faculty and parents in their own lives. In order to fix this, parents and learning leaders must get to the point where their intention to make the world better through our children supersedes their excuses for not raising their own standards.

Failure is an unwillingness to give up what you don't need.

The hypocrisy of educational rhetoric is not lost on the youth of today. It's time to stop pretending that we want better education, it's time to start *being* better examples so that we can hold our children to a higher standard.

Be an adaptable learning organization

The irony of our learning system is how poorly it learns. The number one problem that organizations and individuals face today is in their ability to adapt to change.

We don't know exactly how our economy is going to evolve, but we do know that the pace of change is accelerating and that even the acceleration is accelerating. We have to give up this notion that school must be in massive brick buildings, broken up into classrooms organized by age and subject etc, etc.

We need a completely new, scalable, open learning system that can adapt over Christmas break. This scares many people who crave the stability and security and certainty that come with established institutions. But if you want to observe the greatest suffering in the civilized world, take a look at our most 'established' institutions.

Is that what you want our children's world to look like?

Is that the life that you want for them?

The 3 R's

The designers of our education system had this part right. We do need reading, writing and arithmetic.

This does not mean that we need calculus and Shakespeare as requirements. It's useful to understand their existence and contribution, but not to spend a whole year trying to *know* them at the cost of *understanding* more.

This notion of forcing all our students to study science and literature is like forcing every student to be an athlete.

With the right exposure, we'll create even more Einstein's, Shakespeare's and Phelps.

Learning happens to us when we're doing something else

The best motivation to learn, the best time to learn, and the best way to learn is because you NEED it. The learning's that have truly soaked into my bones are the ones that I developed because I needed them.

There is certainly a base laying phase...perhaps the first few years of education, but we must transition into a project based approach where the reason for me to learn is connected to a bigger project that I am engaged in.

This can happen with projects big and small. Build a rocket with your child. But don't just build the rocket; use it as a time to figure out ballistics, art, and event planning. How high will this rocket fly? What does 675' look like? Let's go measure it out on the street. How long will it take the rocket to get to maximum height? Then what will happen? How will the parachute deploy? How long will it take to reach ground? Where will it land if the wind is blowing 5 knots from the east? Given that, when and where should we launch it to maximize our ability to recover it? How could we decorate the rocket? How could we share the launch with others? Where should they watch from? How should we promote it? Where and when should we do it? Who could we partner with?

You see where I'm going here. We can turn a simple project into an event that enables all members of the team to contribute in powerful ways and for learning to just happen as a consequence of creating and exploring and sharing.

The possibilities are endless. We could spend a week on the rocket project, perhaps even a few weeks and truly learn more about math, physics, art, marketing, leadership and team work than some students learn in 12 years. AND they'll remember it. It will get in their bones and years later it will factor into their ability to appreciate and understand their world.

Understand vs know

This is slightly overlapping with a previous post, but it bears repeating. Traditional schools are designed to get students to know things. I took chemistry, history, physics, Calculus, etc....I remember very little about chemistry or calculus, ok, probably nothing. In fact it has only been through personal curiosity that I have been able to develop an understanding of these subjects.

I have learned more about chemistry for instance watching 10 hours of YouTube videos with our 5 and 6 year old daughters than a year of high school chemistry that included some 300 hours of classroom and study time. What a waste. We have to stop kidding ourselves and stop wasting valuable lifetime.

Our goal needs to be to develop a curiosity and a broad understanding of all facets of life so that the student can discover the facets that capture them. Students don't have to *know everything*, in fact they can't, but it is useful to *understand a lot of things*.

On that note...

10,000 hours

I heard a coach tell a story about a middle-aged client who was unhappy with their career. The coach asked them what they wanted to do. I forget what they picked, but the coach then asked them, "well, how long would it take you to get good enough at that to earn a living from it" The client said something like 10 years, but I can't start over because I'm too old.

The coach asked them, "If you don't pursue this, how old will you be in 10 years, and if you do pursue this, how old will you be in 10 years?" The moral of course is that it's never too late to begin to get really really good at something. The other moral though is that it's a shame to wake up as a middle aged person and NOT be really really good at *something*.

Malcolm Gladwell popularized the 'discovery' that it takes around 10,000 hours or 10 years to become expert at something. Leaving aside for now the quality of those hours and the person's inherent talent (I'll get to these later, don't worry) the premise is that you actually pick something and stick with it long enough to become expert. School doesn't support this because there is very little time and too few avenues to do it.

My point is that whether it ends up being THE thing or not, it is a shame that we ALL don't get to our 18th birthday being really really good at something. It seems to happen more by accident than on purpose.

Talent

Part of learning to BE is learning what we were designed for. I don't buy that some people were born with more talent than others. I believe that we ALL were born with talent, but only a few actually discover theirs. We must create the space for students to discover their talent.

I hear adults say that it can take a lifetime. Perhaps. But it's more probable that most people get smothered by a system that values sitting straight, facing forward and memorization more than developing talent and creativity.

I mourn for the immeasurable talent and creativity that lies under the avalanche of school conditioning and memories.

Our intention is to create a learning environment and experience that provides all students with the ability to develop the character and satisfaction that result from finding their niche and applying extreme amounts of passion and discipline.

We can't do anything we set our minds to

The corollary to the 10,000-hour rule is that we are naturally great in a somewhat narrow area. Applying 10,000 hours of effort in an area that we are not designed for will make us no match for the person who IS talented in that area, AND applies themselves for '10,000 hours'.

Rudy Ruettiger, from the famed football movie 'Rudy' was a 5'6" student at Notre Dame who was hell bent on making the Varsity team. His effort level and commitment made him a contribution to the team, and it makes for a great underdog hero story.

But these kinds of stories mislead us. Yes, Rudy made the team (barely), but in the game of football there are players with talent AND work ethic, and when the mislead Rudy's 'drive their geese to the wrong market' it doesn't tend to end well.

The world is going from broad to narrow. From an inch deep and a mile wide, to an inch wide and a mile deep. Our individual and collective prosperity depends upon not only our effort and heart but where we apply it.

It is far, far better to apply Rudy like effort in *your* domain of talent than it is in someone else's.

Ideas worth spreading

If you haven't been to TED.com yet, make a point of it. TED stands for Technology, Education and Design. They hold conferences where a wide range of remarkable 'experts' entertain, inform and inspire the world with their unique perspectives.

The 'talks' are short, and in the space of 5 to 20 minutes you can be exposed to the best thinkers and communicators in the world. They will share with you, their 'ideas worth spreading', and hopefully you will have your mind opened further than it was and become inspired.

TED talks are an incredibly powerful tool for developing a broad and inclusive understanding of our world. Think back if you can to one of those in class films. Can you remember the tech student threading the projector? Now imagine thousands and thousands of the world's best teachers, thought leaders and presenters from literally around the world just a click away. Oh, and one more thing…they're free!

TED talks are perhaps one of the best and most economical teaching aids ever.

18

If you are looking for a way to supplement your child's worldview AND to manage TV in your house (if you haven't killed your TV yet), try requiring your children to watch a TED talk before they can watch regular TV.

Cloud

TED.com is just one of many powerful and emerging examples of free education in the 'cloud.'

The cloud makes it possible to access live and archived lessons from the best of the best.

The cloud enables live access to incredible learning events that are popping up every day.

The cloud enables access to other students and classes around the world and the possibility of learning to collaborate with global partners in the 3rd grade!

The digital age school must leverage the cloud extensively.

Check out www.kahnacademy.com or try this TED talk on cloud based education http://www.ted.com/talks/sugata_mitra_build_a_school_in_the_cloud.html

Kill your Television

Lest I forget to mention this, kill your TV, or at least bend it to your will. TV has become one giant anxiety producing commercial that trains people to believe that they aren't enough and don't have enough.

TV constantly reminds its viewers that we cannot trust, that we are not safe, and that we are powerless.

THE greatest single change you can make in your home if you have not already done it, is to turn off the media insanity and use your television as a learning device that serves you, not vice versa.

This change will immediately bring the anxiety level of your home down several notches. It will increase true family connection and communication. It will stop the constant hypnosis that you need more food, drugs, alcohol, and stuff to be happy.

And all of that will increase your ability to take a deep breath and get in touch with what you really want for yourself.

Happy Days went off the air 30 years ago, and as the saying goes, "you can't go home again."

Turn off your television and turn on your child's sense of self.

We've become too PC (politically correct)

I'm not supposed to say that TV is a waste of life because it might offend those who watch too much TV. If that offends you it is because it is true for you. I've come to understand through self-examination and coaching that there is nothing I can say to most people that is as bad as what they tell themselves.

Someone can call me a name, but the truth is that I've called myself worse. And if it hurts, it's because it's probably true. If it's not true then it shouldn't hurt. Yes, we need to raise our children to be tolerant and respectful, but word policing addresses the symptom, not the cause.

Politically correct speech has gotten to the point where we're afraid to participate in conversations for fear of saying the 'wrong thing', or saying it in the 'wrong way'.

Innovation has taken a back seat to politically correct speech as an excuse to not deal with real issues. It's a great delay tactic, but I can't see how it's made society any better.

We're taking ourselves way too seriously.

Be in touch with nature often

There is a natural pattern to everything in life including we humans. We ARE nature, yet as a consequence of conquering it we have developed the illusion that we are somehow separate from it. And this has lead to the tragic sense that we are also separate from each other, which is the enabler of countless neglect and exploitation.

SEASONS

SPRING

WINTER — ┼ — SUMMER

FALL

The answers we need exist in THE system that has been in successful and continuous existence for billions of years. Our 'successes' of the last 100 years have not changed this fact.

If the resources to create our 'stuff' come from *other* countries whose environments are being destroyed, then it is *we* who are destroying *our* environment. Nature is not just in our backyard, or our country, or the 'pretty places'…it's everywhere all the time.

There is no excuse for not *understanding* what's inside our food and our stuff or where it *really* comes from. It is impossible for a democratic society to self govern if it doesn't have a real understanding of natural consequences. This can only come from significant and meaningful interaction with nature.

Meditation

If you want some clues about what we need to include in a new school design, look to where adults are struggling. I'm not sure how many books, DVD's and apps there are to assist adults in calming their minds, to stay in the present, or to access their innate wisdom, but it's in the thousands.

Learning to slow down, to reflect, and to really feel is a powerful skill. The reason that adults struggle with this is due in large part to the fact that they have had very little practice. And by the time adults realize they need to slow down, it is often nearly impossible, so most give up and thankfully, [sarcasm] big pharma and happy hour are there to help.

Our children are blank slate learning machines. As early as possible is the right time to assist them in developing a high level of mental and emotional control.

While we're on the subject of health struggles…

Power Nap

The science on this is irrefutable. Astronauts and pilots have been tested after short naps and have been found to be 34% more effective and 100% more alert. If I offered you the opportunity to invest $100 every day and double your money, how could you pass that up?

Think about the lesson here. Take a 20-minute nap and the next 4 hours are 34% more effective, a 4:1 return! How many places can you observe adults sacrificing long—term health for the sake of short-term gains? And what are the consequences hours, days, weeks, and years later?

Napping may sound unnatural, or indulgent or weak, but it's not. What's unnatural is to ignore our bodies, the need for restoration, and to continually trade the important for the seemingly urgent.

Like meditation [and they could be combined], napping is a little habit with a big return. But learning it later in life is more difficult. If napping was part of your normal routine for the first 18 years of your life, I'm betting that you wouldn't balk at it now.

Navy Seals nap, Winston Churchill napped, JFK napped, Thomas Edison napped. Maybe that's why it's called power napping.

Nutrition

The food that we put in our bodies affects mood, mental clarity, concentration, and more. Most of the food that is available to us is processed, and even if it isn't pure sugar, it acts like it. We are chronically inflaming ourselves with toxic stuff that tries to pass as food. The aggregate result of which is sickness, obesity and fatigue. And to counter the sleepy effect of these foods we wash them down with ever-greater quantities of sugar drinks, caffeine and other stimulants.

And then we wonder why ADHD and a host of other attention and hyperactivity issues are on the rise.

Yes, processed food tastes great, and that's why it's so addictive, but it's killing us in the long-term, and preventing our kids from learning in the short-run.

The behavioral difference between kids that eat only whole foods and kids that eat processed foods is night and day. Based upon observation of kid's nutrition and behavior I'd say that over 50% of teacher (and parent) energy is spent managing the consequences of poor nutrition, including their own!

Don't believe me? Try a month eating like our primal ancestors and watch what happens.

School design must not only incorporate whole food nutrition as a given, it should instill the habit of whole food nutrition in the student, so that the adult doesn't have to spend the rest of their lives dieting, fighting their addiction to sugar and stimulants, and eventually succumbing to cancer and heart disease.

And so our society doesn't go bankrupt from healthcare costs.

Fitness

Gym class memories are a factor in why people avoid exercise. At an early age many students learn that exercise shorts + T-shirts = failure. Let's face it, not everyone has the athletic gift just as not everyone has the musical gift. But everyone can exercise and everyone needs the benefits and habit of regular exercise.

Fitness and sport are two different things. Students deserve to learn how to exercise properly and sustainably for life. A proper school should instill this powerful lifelong habit by making it FUN.

Sports

Trying to support a wide range of sports doesn't make sense. Sports require enormous resources and they only benefit a small population of the school. I love sports, but club teams outside of school make much more sense. They allow the school to focus on its learning mission and the athlete to specialize and choose.

Don't get me wrong. I think that sports are an incredible learning opportunity, but school sponsored activities like sports address just a small slice of the extracurricular activities that a student can participate in.

The only way that I see sports making sense in a school is if you incorporate a particular sport that ALL of the students participate in.

Learning Evolution

There is a sequence to introducing new concepts; explore, play, add rigor. Montessori has this right because it allows children to explore the materials at their own pace, and to engage in learning play.

After comfort and familiarity have been established students can then move to more and more rigor. This develops confidence, curiosity, and self-awareness that 'jumping' right in does not.

No more teachers

My best and most memorable teachers (sadly they are too few) were not really teachers so much as leaders. And that's what we really need, learning leaders.

Schools like to say that they recruit the best teachers in each subject. To me the best math teacher is the best presenter, not necessarily the most accomplished mathematician.

When it comes time to explain math to my daughters, I want them to hear from someone who is gifted at presentation. But we can't all have THAT teacher 'in-house' for math or for any other subject for that matter.

What I really want my daughters to spend their time with is a learning leader, a learning coach; someone to guide and support their learning process and nurture their interests and talents.

Leadership is about creating space for accomplishment. The best coaches of all time have not necessarily been the subject experts, but they were experts when it came to holding their team to high standards and giving them room to make mistakes and find their highest contribution.

18

Education degrees and state teaching certificates do not tell me if someone is a gifted learning leader, we need to create the space for a new breed of educator who hold themselves to high standards in every area of their lives, and who act as learning coaches, facilitators, and leaders.

Learning leadership

There is a cycle to learning leadership.

1. At first the student needs specific instruction to understand the basics, often delivered lecture style.
2. Then we move to a more interactive phase where the student is given a task to perform in front of the coach and the coach provides real time feedback.
3. After a while the student can practice more independently with occasional coach support.
4. And finally the student is able to 'fly on their own'.

LEARNING LEADERSHIP

FACILITATE

DIRECT ——————▶ SUPPORT

DELEGATE

18

I heard a powerful story about this dynamic. As I remember it, there was a study done with two college classes for a semester. The first classroom, I'll call them Classroom "A", was taught for the entire semester in the lecture style (see the first step in the learning cycle above).

In Classroom "B" the students also began with the lecture style. They sat in straight rows, faced front and listened to their professor.

Then after a couple weeks of this the professor changed the classroom to a "U" shape with the professor sitting at the 'head' of the "U". During this period the class was much more interactive.

A few weeks later professor "B" changed the seating yet again, this time to a circle. During this period the professor faded into the group and only spoke when there was a question they couldn't answer on their own.

One day toward the end of the semester, the students of both Class A and B arrived outside their respective classrooms to find a note on the door. The note read something like, "Something has come up, I will not be able to make it to class today", and was signed by their professor.

The students of Classroom "A" predictably rejoiced at their newfound free time and scattered. The students of Classroom "B" however reacted much differently. They went into the room and took a seat in the circle and got to work…just like they were taught to.

The students in classroom "B" didn't just learn about a subject, they learned to learn. They learned to take initiative and they learned to lead.

What a powerful example of a small change that makes a big difference.

You get 10 minutes

Just in case you didn't get the insanity of lecturing, here's one more fact for you.

If you study the best practices of public speaking and presenting you will learn that audiences tune out somewhere between 9 and 10 minutes UNLESS there is a significant shift in the presentation such as changing the presenter's voice, showing a video clip etc. This has been studied extensively and the time frame is shortening, not lengthening.

If your audience tunes out after 10 minutes, how can we tolerate a school design that offers 12 straight years x 5 subject lectures per day and expect our children learn? The answer of course is that we can't.

Group accomplishment

The best way to learn is by engaging in meaningful projects with real deliverables, accountability and review. (Just like real life)

During the first period, the students gather as a large group and go over the fundamentals they will need to accomplish the project; the scope, the objective, resources, important concepts etc.

Then, along with their project mentor, the students make decisions about how to divide the work along areas of team member strengths.

Then it's time to dive in and get to work on the project. As they work through the project, they learn what they need to learn as they go.

At the end of the project period the teams will present their result to a live audience who will provide real feedback.

And finally there will be an intense review and feedback period designed to accelerate learning.

In my 20 years as a CEO I can confidently say that an adult's ability to truly give and receive feedback and incorporate it quickly is beyond weak.

18

Group work should form the bulk of student work beginning at the earliest ages possible in order to give our children an advantage that most of us were not given,

Always begin with the prosperous adult in mind

Collaboration is not cheating

I heard yet another story recently of a student caught 'cheating' who in shame later attempted suicide. This story and ones like are a crime. I'm not justifying cheating, though given the emphasis on grades and de-emphasis on substantive learning I can certainly understand it. I doubt that there are many among us who did not at least peek at someone else's paper during a test or a quiz at some point along the line.

All of this individual study and testing sends a message that accomplishment is a solo act. In the real world, nothing could be further from the truth. Significant accomplishment *always* requires a team.

In the real world if I have to make a board presentation, I pull in my team and we split up the work. Spreadsheets, research, outline, content, graphic presentation and more…we divvy it up based upon our strengths. And the same goes for the presentation.

School makes the mistake of not teaching this from day one. Life is a team sport; school must reflect life, exactly.

…which leads to another important point…

Ethics

Students cheat. And not a little, a lot. And not just the poor students, the 'good' students do too, a lot. Students know that they will forget what they are tested on. They know that the system is a game, and 'cheating' is just part of 'gaming' the system.

Is it any wonder that these children become adults who look the other way when they see people 'gaming' the system?

Is it any wonder when these children become adults who often decide something like, "if you can't beat em join em"?

Is it any wonder that these children have become the adults who have elected politicians who 'sell' their votes to lobbyists?

It's all connected. Our children ARE our future. We owe it to them and to ourselves to start them out with the right habits and behaviors.

We can't raise them in a corrupt system and expect them to act ethically later.

Integrity

While we're on the subject of ethics we should mention its cousin integrity. Integrity is not morals. Integrity is when our actions and our intentions are aligned. It is when we do what we say and we say what we do.

The most remarkable companies and people have the most integrated character. You may not love what they stand for, but you can't help notice their magnetic pull.

People are drawn to their focus and their certainty and opportunities seem to just 'land in their laps'. And this phenomenon is available to all of us on any size stage.

But this phenomenon is difficult to produce in ourselves if we lose touch with what we stand for and we never really get a grasp on what our greatest contributions are or how to hone them, market them and get credit for them.

We want our children to have integrated character, so that they can focus their energies and surround themselves with the right people and opportunities, which are the ingredients of a great and prosperous life.

Project group learning mentors

Mentors are profoundly important. I can recall exact conversations with a handful of influential mentors in my life some 30 years after the fact, yet I'm not sure I can remember the words of many of my teachers. Every successful person I have met has at least one mentorship story.

Each story is different and random, but we can create the conditions for it to happen on purpose. The best approach is to expose students to a wide range of adults in real group work situations.

Useful and memorable wisdom will be inevitable.

Class size

Class size is relative. I've been in giant lecture halls and heard a presenter that felt like they were having a conversation with ME. And I've been in room with 5 people and wanted to sleep while the presenter spoke. What we need is quality of interaction.

The United States already spends more per student than most other countries yet in many cases gets inferior results. If we were to hire more teachers to decrease class size, education spending would likely double and not necessarily get better.

Hiring more teachers isn't necessary. Here is a better idea…

Engage the village

A number of years ago I participated in a program in Boston called Citizen Schools. The idea was that adult leaders lead a project for students participating in their after school program.

Each week for a number of weeks I lead a group of students who had chosen from a menu of project choices and adult leaders. Some worked with lawyers and presented in court, some built a racecar, etc.

It was a phenomenally rewarding experience for me and for the students. I'd venture to say that for those students, this after school program is among their most impactful school memories.

Adult leaders like you and I have as much to learn from this process, as they have to learn from us. If each of us had the opportunity to mentor a project for one week per year, each school could create a learning leader roster that exceeds the student body and reduce the student teacher ratio for free!

There is a triangle of interdependency; parents, students and business leaders. We all need each other, we can all learn from each other and there are plenty of us to go around. We don't lack money, we lack intention.

Parents must walk the talk

What we do at school is only half of the equation. Parents must back the school's play. When I was a kid in school I remember a couple of parents who weren't very mature, and came to the 'aid' (unjustifiably) of their children repeatedly. The damage to their child's understanding of consequences was extensive.

As a parent myself I've observed this from a new angle and it's generally clear that when parents get upset at teachers unjustly it's because the school is insisting on some behavior that is not demonstrated by the parents at home. The parents are really just embarrassed.

Parents need to be all in, not just for their child's learning but also for their own as well.

How long should a school day be?

The best creators in the world can't create or practice for much more than 4 to 6 high quality hours, and that's probably stretching it. Extending the school day to 'increase' learning is a myth.

This extra time should be used for focused extra curricular accomplishment.

Another reason to shorten the school day is to allow real time for learning leaders to prepare. We can't expect a high level of energy, creativity and personalization from teachers who don't have time to plan and reflect.

Again, I'm not recommending leisure; I'm differentiating 'class time' from other powerful development activities.

Scheduling and breaks

When an athlete trains, they periodize. That is they train in micro blocks that build in intensity and finish with a recovery phase. Each micro block makes up the macro-training period.

School should model after this. School and athletic training for months in a row without a clear beginning and end dulls the training effect. With a regular rhythm of 4 to 6 weeks the students can rest up and reflect between periods to increase their effort and focus during each micro cycle.

Every world-class athlete trains this way; we can give our students the same advantage.

Learning and humiliation are the same

The definition of both is to act outside of one's self image. Most people fear public speaking for example. The reason is that the essence of all human action is to manifest our identity, or at least the one that we think we have. And getting up to speak could expose incompetence.

I'm not suggesting that we ridicule one another to learn. What I'm saying is that our concern for being embarrassed stagnates growth and learning.

School must create the expectation that we will all take risks and we will all respect and support each other for taking them. Risk not conformity needs to be the currency of 'cool'.

Tough Love and hard things

Part in parcel with true learning is tough love. There will be reluctance, that's to be expected, but the only way out is through.

Students must be held accountable to attempt and succeed at doing 'hard things', often.

The most rewarding life accomplishments are not easy, they're hard.

The greatest contributions to society were not easy, they were hard.

In fact, in many cases our greatest accomplishments seemed impossible at first. But the victors began with a first step and continued with the expectation that their commitment must exceed their doubts and their fears.

I want our children to learn to face their fears early and often so that they can develop the resilience necessary to prosper in a world that is in constant and rapid change.

I want our children to face their fears so that they can build their character, and experience the incredible satisfaction of meaningful accomplishment.

18

Borrowed from a recent favorite read, Do Hard Things by Alex and Brett Harris, here is a great list of 'Hard Things';

1. Things that take you out of your comfort zone
2. Things that go beyond what's expected or required
3. Things that are too big to do alone
4. Things that don't pay off immediately
5. Things that go against the crowd

Turn off the lights

When I was young I worked on fishing boats where I learned that it didn't matter if you were the captain or the deckhand, every crewmember was responsible for the boat. The boat was literally the container that separated us from death by very cold water. That experience taught me to treat every environment as if it were my own.

There is a sense of entitlement and separateness that plagues our society. Many people expect to be picked up after and forget that we all live on the same earth and depend upon the same resources.

If I walk out of a room and leave the lights on, I may not pay the 'bill' directly, but MY / OUR resources are used up just the same.

There is no 'Them'. We are all one and the lesson of our time is to remember this and become one again.

Everyone stands watch

Another fish story.

When you're at sea for an extended period of time, everyone must stand watch. That is, everyone must take a turn at each job; helm, lookout, galley etc.

There is no better time or place than school to teach our children to understand what it takes to make an organization work and to take ownership in it's success.

The ideal school will engage students in its operation. Every student should develop a sense of ownership and responsibility; galley duty, maintenance, book keeping, landscaping etc. are fantastic opportunities for learning that are plentiful, real, and free.

Manners

Why manners are not taught I can only guess. It's not hard to learn them and the value is priceless.

Resolving conflict

Hoo boy. We adults stink at this. We're awesome at dictating, escaping, compromising, and even hibernating. Anything but actually resolving conflicts without lawyers and guns.

One thing is for certain, when two or more people coexist, there will be conflicts. There are a number of ways to teach this and it needs to be woven into the fabric of the learning experience to the point where it becomes as second nature as driving a car.

It's only difficult when you are allowed to grow up with the pretense that you can avoid conflict and prosper.

Teaching conflict resolution to children while they are young, and making it a regular practice will give them the ability to not have to be slaves to the adult habits of dictation, escape, toleration, and hibernation.

18

By their 18th birthday, the student should be able to enter the world as a powerful contributor. The real world should not be a stranger to them, nor them to it, and they should be confident in their ability to thrive in it.

If college or some other form of continued study makes sense, fine. But students shouldn't be going to college to 'figure it out', or to 'grow up'.

18 years old is the school's delivery date to supply society with an adult fully capable of prospering.

Education never ends

My college has been asking me for money ever since I graduated. I haven't counted how many communications I have received asking for money, but I can count exactly how many invitations I have received to continue my learning; ZERO.

Education doesn't end after 'school' and the student's participation shouldn't either. My idea for an ideal school is that it have a space for the student to continue learning and contributing forever.

College, one more time for good measure

College is extremely relevant to education design because schools are designed to generate high-standardized test scores, which are used as the basis for acceptance to college.

We must decouple college from education design or we are doomed to repeat past and current mistakes. College admissions officers are not the 'customer'; our children who represent our future society are the customers.

The street value of the college diploma has been steadily dropping for the last couple of decades, and the pace of decline is accelerating.

There are two giant breakdowns here;

First, the economics are negative for most graduates. Just take the tuition and the lost opportunity cost of 4 + years and compare it to the present value of the future income stream and Warren Buffet wouldn't buy that stock.

Second, the economics are made worse by the fact that many grads sit on the sidelines either as unemployed or underemployed for several years post college.

18

Too many parents try to rationalize the poor economics with statements like -"College is where you grow up…best years of your life…they'll make great connections…." I argue that there are more intentional and economical ways to 'grow up'.

Students get caught in the rationalization trap as well by advertising that sells degrees as tickets to 'better futures.'

I am not, I repeat not, saying that college is bad in and of itself or a bad idea for ALL students.

My point is that for most students the economics don't work and the result is a one-way ticket to debt and technopeasanthood where graduates become commodity workers until their service is automated or outsourced to a lower labor market.

The antidote to becoming a commodity in any industry is to develop a powerful sense of self, coupled with the ability to reinvent your offer and transact on ones own behalf.

The market pays only for satisfaction, not for degrees. Only the intensity of our children's intention to be powerful contributors will ensure their prosperity. So their education had better develop this in them, or college won't matter.

This may sound like only a money argument, it's not, four years of life is a very, very heavy price to pay. The value of four years of a student's life dwarfs the tuition cost, especially if the reason for being in college isn't crystal clear.

What would you pay to get back 4 years of your life?

The answer is to prepare our children to be ready to prosper by 18. If college makes sense, great, but we shouldn't cross our fingers and hope that college will fill in the voids of, and make up for the lost time in, K-12 education.

The Vision

Abraham Lincoln said this about education:

> "The philosophy of the classroom in this generation will be the philosophy of politics, government, and life in the next."

I agree. And when I look at the philosophy of politics and government and even more importantly the cold hard reality of life today, I don't like what I see. If we educate our children as we did today's leadership, we knowingly sentence them to even greater suffering.

However well intentioned our efforts have been, the result is that we have become imprisoned by our willingness to accept the status quo. A society as sick and stressed as ours has become is not free. And as our society goes, there too go our children.

Benjamin Franklin said that the purpose of education is to produce "self determined free agents", that is our intention as well. Our intention is to create an educational environment where our children develop the self-awareness, character and skills they need to become remarkable contributors.

For more information about how to be a part of the next generation of education, visit www.TobyLaVigne.com

Toby LaVigne – Jupiter, FL

Toby is a problem solver, an intuitive coach, a keen observer of people's strengths, and an enthusiastic change agent. It has always been Toby's dream to build a school that would fill the tremendous gap between what school teaches and how the real world works. But his goal is to not just teach, the goal is to forge remarkable contributors for the sake of our children.

- Husband and father of two girls
- Colby College undergrad Cornell MBA

- 20 year technology CEO
- 17 year YPO member and active contributor
- 2-time YPO International Best of the Best award winner
- Inventor and patent holder -Commercial Cloud Printing
- Founder of HubCast.com
- Boards: YPO, Boys and Girls Clubs of America, Ducks Unlimited, and the First Tee

Random facts

1. Began his career as a commercial fisherman
2. Built his first house by hand
3. Was voted most ethical by his business school class
4. Wants to be in the Blue Man Group when he grows up
5. CrossFit enthusiast, former top ranked triathlete

The ideas and perspectives expressed in this book are the result of my personal educational experience, my experience as a CEO, my experience as a parent, and extensive study on the subject. The following books and videos highlight some of the influential, inspirational, and informative sources of my study. I have listed them here for your convenience.

Resources

Great Books about education

- Doing School: How We Are Creating a Generation of Stressed-Out, Materialistic, and Miseducated Students by Denise Clark Pope
- An Ethic of Excellence: Building a Culture of Craftsmanship with Students by Ron Berger
- Disrupting Class: How Disruptive Innovation Will Change the Way the World Learns by Clayton Christensen, Curtis Johnson, Michael Horn
- Unschooling Rules: 55 Ways to Unlearn What We Know About Schools and Rediscover Education by Clark Aldrich
- Do Hard Things: A Teenage Rebellion Against Low Expectations
- Antifragility: Things that gain from Disorder by Nassim Nicholas Taleb

TED Talks at TED.com

- Sir Ken Robinson – How Schools kill creativity
- Logan Laplante – Hackingschool Makes Me Happy
- Sugatra Mitra – Build a school in the cloud

- Salman Kahn – Let's use video to reinvent education
- John Hunter – Teaching with the world peace game

Movie

- Finding Joe A wonderful and inspirational movie about the 'heroes' journey that we are all meant to experience.